The Cure 1

MARTIN MEYER

Text Copyright © Martin Meyer

All rights reserved. No part of this guide may be reproduced in any form without permission in writing from the publisher except in the case of brief quotations embodied in critical articles or reviews.

Legal & Disclaimer

Legal & Disclaimer

The information contained in this book is not designed to replace or take the place of any form of medicine or professional medical advice. The information in this book has been provided for educational and entertainment purposes only.

The information contained in this book has been compiled from sources deemed reliable, and it is accurate to the best of the Author's knowledge; however, the Author cannot guarantee its accuracy and validity and cannot be held liable for any errors or omissions. Changes are periodically made to this book. You must consult your doctor or get professional medical advice before using any of the suggested remedies, techniques, or information in this book.

Upon using the information contained in this book, you agree to hold harmless the Author from and against any damages, costs, and expenses, including any legal fees potentially resulting from the application of any of the information provided by this guide. This disclaimer applies to any damages or injury caused by the use and application, whether directly or indirectly, of any advice or information presented, whether for breach of contract, tort, negligence, personal injury, criminal intent, or under any other cause of action.

You agree to accept all risks of using the information presented inside this book. You need to consult a professional medical practitioner in order to ensure you are both able and healthy enough to participate in this program.

Table of Contents

Section A: Introduction to ADHD   10

Chapter 1: The Science of ADHD   10

What is ADHD?   10
ADHD and Executive Functions (EF)   11
Types of ADHD   12
1. Inattentive Type   12
2. Hyperactive-Impulsive Type   13
3. Combined Type   13

Occurrence of ADHD   14

Chapter 2: Signs and Symptoms   15

Concentration and Focusing Issues   16
Hyper focus   17
Disorganized and Forgetful   18
Impulsivity   18
Emotional Problems   19
No Rest and Hyperactivity   20
Conditions Related alongside ADHD   20

Chapter 3: Causes   22

Genes   23
Diet and Nutrition   23
Environment   24
Brain Injury   25

Other Causes   25

Chapter 4: Normal Brain vs. ADHD Brain   27

- Brain Size   27
- Structure   29
- Functional   29
- Electrical activity   30
- Chemical   31

Section B: Conventional Treatment   32

Chapter 5: Normal Medication   32

- Some Important things about Medications   33
- Stimulant Medications   34
  - Safety Concerns   35
- Most Common ADHD drugs   36
  - Ritalin, Mehylin, Metadate, Concerta, Daytrana (methylphenidate)   37
  - Adderall (dextroamphetamine and amphetamine)   37
  - Dexedrine (dextroamphetamine)   38
  - Vyvanse (lisdexamfetamine dimesylate)   38
  - Focalin (dexmethylphenidate)   38
  - Aplezin, Wellbutrin, Zyban (buproprion)   38
  - Intuniv, Tenex (guanfacine)   39
  - Catapres (clonidine)   39
  - Strattera   40

Chapter 6: Non-Medical Treatment   42

Exercise	42
Sleep	44
Relaxation techniques	44
Meditation	44
Professional Therapy	45
Talk treatment	45
Marriage and family treatment	46
Psychological behavioral treatment	46
Professional Organizers	46

Section C: Fixing ADHD with Diet — 48

Chapter 7: Food Sensitivities of Patients — 48

Milk and Cheese	49
Wheat, Rye and Barley	49
Candy	50
Soda	51
Frozen Fruits and Vegetables	51
Energy Drinks	51
Seafood	52
Food Allergies in General	52

Chapter 8: The Essential Minerals — 54

Magnesium	54
Zinc	55
Selenium	56
Fish Oil	57

Probiotics — 57
L-Carnitine — 58
ADHD Specific Supplements — 58

Chapter 9: Omega-3 Fatty Acids — 60

What are Omega-3 Fatty Acids? — 60
Omega-3 in Adult ADHD — 61
Why Should You Opt for Omega-3? — 61
Omega-3 vs. Omega-6 fatty acids — 62
- Ratio of Omega-6 to Omega-3 — 62
- Omega-6 and Omega-3 fatty acids compete — 62
- Effect of Omega-6 on ADHD — 63

Fish for Omega-3? — 63
Scientific Dosage — 64
Dosage for Adults — 64
Dosage for Children — 65

Chapter 10: Foods to Avoid — 66

Ice Cream — 66
Coffee — 66
Swordfish — 67
Chocolate — 67
Frozen Pizza — 67
Corn — 68
Chips — 68
Squash — 68

Red Meat	69
Cheese	69

Section D: What to Eat? — 71

Chapter 11: ADHD Diet and Nutritional Supplements — 71

Nutrition from Foods	72
A high-protein diet	72
Less basic sugars	72
More unpredictable carbs	72
More omega-3 fatty acids	72
Best Foods for ADHD	73
Apples	73
Goat's Cheese	74
Pears	74
Eggs	74
Nuts	75
Spinach	75
Kiwi	75
Whole Grain Cereals	76

Chapter 12: Vitamins — 77

Vitamin B6	77
Vitamin B12	78
Vitamin B3	78
Other B Vitamins	79

Vitamins A and E	79
Vitamin D	80
Section E: Conclusion	**82**

Section A: Introduction to ADHD

Chapter 1: The Science of ADHD

ADHD is not new; it has been depicted in writing and medicinally recorded for over two centuries. ADHD is a ceaseless condition that can introduce at all levels of seriousness and once in a while happens independent from anyone else. There are three center symptoms, the failure to direct consideration, and the powerlessness to control movement, and trouble with inhibitory conduct bringing about impulsivity. In any case, trouble with directing feelings is frequently an issue also. Note that symptoms of ADHD can fluctuate from every day and hour to hour, keeping in mind numerous youngsters might display these symptoms, it is the level of presentation, the failure to direct them and a level of debilitation, that outcomes in a determination.

What is ADHD?
Attention deficit hyperactivity disorder (ADHD) influences kids and high school students can proceed into adulthood. ADHD is the most ordinarily analyzed mental issue of youngsters. Youngsters with ADHD might be hyperactive and not able control their driving forces. On the other hand they might experience difficulty focusing. These practices meddle with school and home life.

It's more basic in young men than in girls. **Boys are around three times more probable than young ladies** to be determined to have it; however it's not yet comprehended why. It's generally found during the early school years, when a youngster starts to have issues focusing.

Grown-ups with ADHD might experience difficulty overseeing time, being composed, setting objectives, and holding down a vocation. <u>They might likewise have issues with connections, self-regard, and habit.</u>

Kids with ADHD act without considering, are hyperactive, and experience difficulty centering. They might comprehend what's anticipated from them however experience difficulty finishing on the grounds that they can't sit still, focus, or concentrate on subtle elements.

Obviously, all people (especially younger ones) act along these lines on occasion, especially when they're anxious or energized. However, the distinction with ADHD is that manifestations are available over a more drawn out timeframe and happen in diverse settings. They hurt a kid's capacity to work socially, scholastically, and at home.

The uplifting news is that with legitimate treatment, kids with ADHD can figure out how to effectively live with and deal with their indications.

ADHD and Executive Functions (EF)

New research has demonstrated to us that kids and grown-ups with ADHD regularly have shortcomings in the territories of **executive functioning (EF).** Executive functioning is the mental process that permits us to arrange ahead, assess the past, begin and complete an undertaking and deal with our time. <u>Executive functioning aptitudes empower us to: recognize an issue, discover arrangements, compose ourselves, manage our behavior and feelings, control our consideration levels and oppose diversions</u>.

Working memory, a vital piece of executive functioning, is an ability that permits us to keep data in the cerebrum and work with it in the meantime. Working memory straightforwardly affects reading comprehension, composed expression, math aptitudes and the capacity to focus and oppose diversion. Students with ADHD additionally every now and again process data coming in and going out at a slower speed. Youngsters with shortfalls in these regions are often mislabeled as being unmotivated, disobedient, and apathetic.

Types of ADHD

With regards to ADHD, nobody determination or treatment fits completely. Everybody is distinctive. Scientists and specialists have distinguished three sorts. Each has distinctive symptoms, and medicines depend on those symptoms.

These three types of ADHD are

1. <u>Inattentive Type</u>

A patient with this sort must have no less than six of these nine symptoms, and not very many of the symptoms of hyperactive-impulsive sort:

- Not paying consideration on point of interest

- Committing careless errors
- Neglecting to focus and continue on a task
- Not tuning in to someone talking
- Being not able to take after or comprehend guidelines
- Staying away from tasks that include exertion and efforts
- Being occupied
- Being absent minded
- Losing things that are expected to finish tasks.

2. Hyperactive-Impulsive Type

To have this sort, a man needs to have no less than six of these nine symptoms, and not very many of the symptoms of inattentive sort:

- Fidgeting
- Squirming
- Getting up frequently when sitting
- Running or moving at unseemly times
- Experiencing difficulty playing quietly
- Talking excessively
- Talking out of turn or exclaiming
- Hindering
- Frequently "on the go" as though "driven by an engine".

3. Combined Type

This is the most common type of ADHD. People with it have symptoms of both inattentive and hyperactive-impulsive types.

Occurrence of ADHD

ADHD is the most widely recognized mental health issue of adolescence. Thinks about all through the world have reported the event of ADHD in school age kids as being somewhere around **5% and 12%.** This implies by and large there are no less than one to three kids in each class with ADHD. A larger number of young men than young ladies are analyzed at a rate of 3 to 1.

On the other hand, since young ladies are less inclined to show outward hyperactivity and impulsivity, and the same number of ladies as men is analyzed in adulthood, we realize that we miss diagnosing numerous young ladies with ADHD in adolescence. Females with ADHD are just as debilitated in the zones of consideration and social and scholastic issues as guys. Eighty percent of young people who were analyzed as youngsters keep on meeting the criteria for determination, and of those kids, more than sixty percent report kept debilitating symptoms into adulthood.

Chapter 2: Signs and Symptoms

Life can be a balancing act for any adult, but if you find yourself constantly late, disorganized, forgetful, and overwhelmed by your responsibilities, you may have ADHD. Attention deficit disorder affects many adults, and its wide variety of frustrating symptoms can hinder everything from your relationships to your career. But help is available and learning about ADHD is the first step. Once you understand the challenges, you can learn to compensate for areas of weakness and start taking advantage of your strengths.

<u>Attention deficit disorder regularly goes unrecognized all through adolescence</u>. This was especially normal previously, when not very many individuals knew about ADHD. Rather than perceiving your symptoms and recognizing the main problem, your family, educators, or different folks might have marked you a visionary, a fool, a good-for-nothing, a troublemaker, or only an awful understudy.

On the other hand, you might have possessed the capacity to adjust for the symptoms of ADHD when you were young, just to keep running into issues as your obligations increment. The more balls you're attempting to keep in the air seeking after a profession, raising a family, running a family unit the more prominent the interest on your capacities to sort out, center, and try to avoid panicking. This can be trying for anybody, yet in the event that you have ADHD, it can feel out and out unimaginable.

The uplifting news is that, regardless of how it feels, the difficulties of attention deficit disorder are conquerable. With training, support, and a little innovativeness, you can figure out how to deal with the symptoms of grown-up ADHD notwithstanding transforming some of your shortcomings into strength.

In grown-ups, attention deficit disorder frequently looks very not the same as it does in kids—and its symptoms are exceptional for every person. The following classifications highlight normal symptoms of grown-up ADHD. Do your best to distinguish the zones where you encounter trouble. When you pinpoint your most dangerous symptoms, you can begin to take a shot at methodologies for managing the disorder.

Concentration and Focusing Issues

Grown-ups with ADHD frequently experience issues staying centered and taking care of day by day, everyday assignments. For instance, you might be effectively occupied by immaterial sights and sounds, rapidly skip starting with one action then onto the next, or get to be exhausted rapidly. Symptoms in this classification are some of the time neglected on the grounds that they are less ostensibly problematic than the ADD/ADHD symptoms of hyperactivity and impulsivity yet they can be just as troublesome. The symptoms of inattention and fixation challenges include:

- "Daydreaming" without realizing it, even during a discussion

- Amazing distractibility; meandering attention makes it difficult to remain focused
- Trouble focusing or concentrating, for example, while reading or listening to others
- Attempting to finish assignments, even ones that appear to be basic
- Propensity to ignore subtle elements, prompting mistakes or deficient work
- Poor listening abilities; hard time recollecting discussions and taking after directions.

Hyper focus

While you're most likely mindful that individuals with ADHD experience difficulty focusing on errands that aren't intriguing to them, you may not realize that there's another side: an inclination to end up consumed in undertakings that are animating and remunerating. This confusing side effect is called hyper focus.

Hyper focus is really a method for dealing with stress for diversion a method for blocking out the disarray. It can be strong to the point that you get to be unaware of everything going ahead around you. For instance, you might be so fascinated in a book, a TV appears, or your PC that you totally forget about time and disregard the things should be doing.

<u>Hyper focus can be a benefit when directed into beneficial exercises; however it can likewise prompt work and relationship issues if left unchecked.</u>

Disorganized and Forgetful

When you have grown-up ADHD, life frequently appears to be turbulent and wild. Staying composed and in control can be to a great degree testing—as is sorting out what data is pertinent for the current workload, organizing the things you have to do, monitoring assignments and obligations, and dealing with your time. Basic symptoms of complication and absent mindedness include:

- Poor authoritative skills (home, office, work area, or auto is to a great degree muddled and messed)
- Tendency to procrastinate
- Inconvenience beginning and completing undertakings
- Constant delay
- As often as possible overlooking arrangements, responsibilities, and due dates
- Continually losing or losing things (keys, wallet, telephone, records, bills)
- Thinking little of the time it will take you to finish assignment.

Impulsivity

In the event that you experience the ill effects of symptoms in this class, you might experience difficulty repressing your behaviors, remarks, and reactions. You may act before considering, or respond without considering outcomes. You might end up intruding on others, exclaiming remarks, and racing through assignments without reading guidelines. On the off chance that you have impulse issues, being patient is amazingly troublesome. For better or for more awful, you might go headlong into circumstances and end up in conceivably dangerous circumstances. You might battle with controlling driving forces in the event that you:

- Often intrude on others or talk over them
- Have poor restraint
- Exclaim thoughts that are inconsiderate or unseemly without considering
- Have addictive propensities
- Act heedlessly or suddenly without respect for outcomes
- Experience difficulty carrying on in socially fitting routes, (for example, sitting as yet during a long meeting).

Emotional Problems

Numerous grown-ups with ADHD experience serious difficulties their sentiments, especially with regards to feelings such as outrage or disappointment. Regular enthusiastic symptoms of grown-up ADHD include:

- Feeling of underachievement
- Doesn't bargain well with disappointment
- Effectively bothered and worried
- Fractiousness or emotional episodes
- Inconvenience staying roused
- Hypersensitivity to feedback

- Short, regularly touchy, temper
- Low self-regard and feeling of frailty

No Rest and Hyperactivity

Hyperactivity in grown-ups with ADHD can appear to be identical as it does in children. You might be profoundly enthusiastic and ceaselessly "on the go" as though determined by an engine. For some individuals with ADHD, on the other hand, the symptoms of hyperactivity turn out to be more unobtrusive and inner as they become more established. Regular symptoms of hyperactivity in grown-ups include:

- Sentiments of internal eagerness, agitation
- Propensity to go for broke
- Getting exhausted effortlessly
- Dashing thoughts
- Inconvenience sitting still; consistent wriggling
- Longing for energy
- Talking too much
- Doing a million things without a moment's delay.

Conditions Related alongside ADHD

Despite the fact that not generally the situation, a few youngsters might likewise have signs of different issues or conditions nearby ADHD, for example,

- **Tension disorder** – which causes your youngster to stress and be anxious a great part of the time; it

might likewise bring about physical symptoms, for example, a quick pulse, sweating and wooziness
- **Oppositional defiant disorder (ODD)** – this is characterized by negative and troublesome behavior, especially towards power figures, for example, folks and educators
- **Conduct disorder** – this regularly includes a propensity towards exceptionally standoffish behavior, for example, taking, battling, vandalism and hurting individuals or creatures
- Wretchedness
- **Sleep issues** – thinking that it's hard to get the opportunity to sleep around evening time, and having sporadic sleeping examples
- **Autistic spectrum disorder (ASD)** – this influences social connection, correspondence, hobbies and behavior
- **Epilepsy** – a condition that influences the cerebrum and causes rehashed fits or seizures
- **Tourette's syndrome** – a state of the sensory system, portrayed by a mix of automatic clamors and developments called tics
- **Learning challenges** – for example dyslexia

Chapter 3: Causes

Nobody knows without a doubt. ADHD probably stems from interactions between genes and environmental or non-genetic factors.

ADHD regularly keeps running in families. Analysts have found that a significant part of the danger of having ADHD needs to do with genes. Numerous genes are connected to ADHD, and every gene assumes a little part in the disorder. ADHD is exceptionally unpredictable and a hereditary test for diagnosing the disorder is not yet accessible.

Similarly as with every single mental disorder, the careful reason for attention deficit disorder (ADHD) is obscure, so folks ought not to censure themselves for this issue. It is likely that numerous elements assume a part for every situation of ADHD, almost no of which needs to do with particular child rearing or tyke raising abilities.

Specialists trust that sometime in the future, understanding the reasons for the condition will prompt powerful treatments and confirmation is expanding in favor of hereditary foundations for ADHD instead of components of the home environment. Certain parts of a kid's situation might, then again, influence the indication seriousness of ADHD once it is set up.

Some of the main causes known for ADHD are:

Genes

ADHD has a solid hereditary premise in the lion's share of cases, as a youngster with ADHD is four times as prone to have had a relative who was likewise determined to have attention deficit disorder. Right now, scientists are examining a wide range of genes, especially ones included with the cerebrum synthetic dopamine. **Individuals with ADHD appear to have lower levels of dopamine in the mind.**

Youngsters with ADHD who convey a specific variant of a specific quality have more slender cerebrum tissue in the regions of the mind connected with attention. Research into this quality has demonstrated that the distinction is not lasting, be that as it may. As youngsters with this quality grow up, their brains created to an ordinary level of thickness and most ADHD symptoms died down.

Diet and Nutrition

Certain segments of the eating regimen, including nourishment added substances and sugar, can adversely affect behavior. A few specialists trust that sustenance added substances might worsen ADHD. Also, a prevalent view is that refined sugar might be at fault for a scope of strange behaviors.

On the other hand, the conviction that sugar is one of the essential drivers of attention deficit disorder does not have solid backing in the exploration information. While some more established studies did recommend a connection, later research does not demonstrate a connection in the middle of ADHD and sugar. While the jury is still out on whether sugar can add to ADHD symptoms, most specialists now trust that the connection is not a solid one. <u>Basically expelling sugar from a child's eating regimen is unrealistic to altogether affect their ADHD behavior.</u>

A few concentrates additionally recommend that an absence of omega-3 unsaturated fats is connected to ADHD symptoms. These fats are imperative for mental health and capacity, and there is a lot of proof proposing that an insufficiency might add to developmental disorders including ADHD. Fish oil supplements seem to mitigate ADHD symptoms, in any event in a few kids, and might even support their execution at school.

Environment

There might be a connection in the middle of ADHD and maternal smoking. Be that as it may, ladies who experience the ill effects of ADHD themselves will probably smoke, so a hereditary clarification can't be discounted. **By and by, nicotine can bring about hypoxia (absence of oxygen) in utero.**

<u>Lead introduction has additionally been recommended as a donor to ADHD.</u> In spite of the fact that paint no more contains lead, it is conceivable that preschool youngsters who live in more seasoned structures might be presented to poisonous levels of lead from old paint or plumbing that has not been supplanted.

Brain Injury

Brain injury might likewise be a reason for attention deficit disorder in some little minority of kids. This can occur taking after presentation to poisons or physical harm, either before or after conception. Specialists say that head wounds can bring about ADHD-such as symptoms in beforehand unaffected individuals, maybe because of frontal projection harm.

Other Causes

Different reasons have likewise been recommended as having a part in the advancement of ADHD, including:

- Being conceived premature (before the 37th week of pregnancy)
- Having a low birth weight
- Mind harm either in the womb or in the initial couple of years of life
- Drinking liquor, smoking or abusing drugs while pregnant
- Introduction to elevated amounts of poisonous lead at a young age

In any case, the confirmation for a large number of these elements is uncertain, and more research is expected to figure out whether they do actually add to ADHD.

Chapter 4: Normal Brain vs. ADHD Brain

Kids and high school students with ADHD, another study discovers, lag behind others of the same age in how rapidly their brains structure connections inside, and between, key brain systems.

The outcome: <u>less-develop connections between a brain system that controls inside coordinated thought, (for example, daydreaming) and organizes that permit a man to focus on remotely coordinated assignments. That lag in association improvement might clarify why individuals with ADHD get effortlessly occupied or battle to stay focused.</u>

Neuroimaging studies have associated various structural, functional, electrical activity and chemical correlates with attention-deficit hyperactivity disorder (ADHD) in children, adolescents and adults.

Brain Size

One study took a gander at youngsters with and without ADHD over a 10-year period. At different ages, youngsters' brains were filtered utilizing attractive reverberation imaging (MRI). The specialists found that:

- The brains of young men and young ladies with ADHD were 3% to 4% smaller than the brains of youngsters without ADHD.

- Youngsters with more serious ADHD symptoms had smaller frontal flaps, worldly dark matter, caudate core, and cerebellum. These brain locales are included in fixation, motivation control, restraint, and engine movement, which are all issue zones for kids with ADHD. They are talked about in more detail underneath.
- The course of brain improvement in youngsters with and without ADHD was comparable. This proposes changes in the brain happen ahead of schedule being developed.

Different studies have utilized utilitarian MRI (fMRI) to gauge brain actuation while youngsters are performing different errands. These studies have demonstrated that diminishments in brain volume in kids with ADHD are connected with poorer execution on:

- Tests of attention and hindrance
- Measures of behavior

Structure

Brain imaging concentrates on have related auxiliary variations from the norm with ADHD in youngsters and teenagers including:

- Delayed cortical improvement,
- Cortical diminishing
- Decreases in the volume of dark and white matter Reductions in the volume of a few districts of the brain, including: the back substandard vermis; splenium of the corpus callosum; add up to and right cerebral volume; right caudate; right worldwide pallidus; right foremost frontal locale; cerebellum; fleeting projection; and pulvinar.

Brain variations from the norm connected with ADHD in kids and youths might persevere into adulthood. X-ray considers in grown-ups have yielded comparative proof as depicted above as to decrease in the volume of a few areas of the brain, cortical thickness, and dim matter; especially in the frontal cortex of the brain, contrasted and controls; and in addition auxiliary variations from the norm in joining brain cells inside of systems that manage attention and feeling.

Functional

Brain structures embroiled in ADHD compare to brain systems, including some including frontal districts, and some that bolster executive capacity and attention.

Enactment variations from the norm are connected with ADHD in kids, young people and grown-ups, with meta-examinations exhibiting critical actuation decreases in different frontal districts of the brain including the foremost cingulate; dorsolateral prefrontal and substandard prefrontal cortices; and related locales including the basal ganglia, thalamus, and regions of parietal cortex.

Moreover, atypical useful system availability in the default mode organizes (a system of brain locales that are dynamic during resting) has been seen in kids and young people with ADHD.

What's more, there is some confirmation that examples of under-and over-actuation of specific locales of the brain contrast in the middle of kids and young people versus grown-ups, as demonstrated by a meta-examination of 55 fMRI thinks about which analyzed youngsters, youths and grown-ups with ADHD with solid controls.

Electrical activity

A meta-investigation of overall studies reported that quantitative electroencephalography (EEG; the recording of electrical movement along the scalp) might be utilized to distinguish changes in brain electrical action. An expansion in the theta/beta (two EEG recurrence groups) proportion was seen in all studies incorporated into the review. Further exploration is required to substantiate EEG discoveries for use as a biomarker in ADHD diagnosis. Individual EEG designs connected with ADHD are under right on time examination for utility in customizing neuro-feedback conventions computer-helped preparing to self-direct brainwave action as non-pharmacological treatment alternatives for ADHD.

Chemical

Deferred development of certain dopaminergic neural pathways has been seen in youngsters and teenagers with ADHD as well as a lopsidedness in the levels of both dopamine and noradrenaline in the brains of kids, youths and grown-ups with ADHD contrasted and sound controls. Dopamine and noradrenaline have been ensnared in affecting impulsivity, and dopamine in impacting inattention.

Developing confirmation additionally proposes conceivable parts for other flagging frameworks in the neurobiology of ADHD. Insufficiencies in glutamate motioning in a few districts of the brain might have a modulatory part in grown-ups with ADHD. Furthermore, polymorphisms in the serotonin transporter quality have been connected with differential reaction to ADHD treatment, and the vicinity of comorbid conduct disorder in kids and teenagers with hyperkinetic disorder (an option portrayal of ADHD).

Section B: Conventional Treatment

Chapter 5: Normal Medication

Doctors regularly recommend medications to lessening ADHD indications. Pretty much as each case varies, not each individual will take the same medications. Treatment methodologies can likewise differ in the middle of kids and grown-ups. It's essential to talk about all ADHD treatment choices with your doctor to pick up the best results.

Drug is a vital piece of your ADHD treatment. Numerous sorts of medications can be utilized to control side effects of the disorder.

Drug can <u>lessen</u> side effects of hyperactivity, distractedness, and impulsivity in kids and grown-ups with ADHD. However, medications accompany side effects and risks—and are not by any means the only treatment alternative. Whether you're the guardian or the patient, it's essential to take in the truths about ADHD solution so you can settle on an educated decision about what's best for you.

You and your doctor will cooperate to make sense of which pharmaceutical is a good fit for you, alongside the ideal dose (amount) and plan (how frequently or when you have to take it). It might require some investment to make sense of that thing.

Some Important things about Medications

Settling on ADHD medication decisions can be troublesome; however getting your research done makes a difference. The principal thing to comprehend is precisely what the medications for ADHD can and can't do. ADHD drug might enhance the capacity to focus, control motivations, plan ahead, and complete assignments. <u>However, it isn't an enchantment pill that will alter the greater part of your issues.</u>

Notwithstanding when the prescription is working, a man with ADHD may at present battle with absent mindedness, enthusiastic issues, and social ungainliness, or a grown-up with disruption, distractibility, and relationship troubles. That is the reason it's so vital to likewise roll out way of life improvements that incorporate standard work out, a solid eating routine, and adequate rest.

Prescription doesn't cure ADHD. It can ease manifestations while it's being taken, however once solution stops, those side effects return. Likewise, ADHD drug works preferred for some over for others. A few individuals experience sensational change while others encounter just humble additions. Since every individual reacts diversely and unusually to pharmaceutical for ADHD, its utilization ought to dependably be customized to the individual and nearly monitored by a doctor. At the point when prescription for ADHD is not precisely monitored, it is not so much effective but rather more dangerous.

Medications come in various forms:

- **Short-acting (prompt discharge)** - These produce results rapidly. They can wear off rapidly, as well. You might need to take these few times each day.
- **Intermediate Acting** - These last more than short-acting variants.
- **Long-acting forms** - You may just need to take this kind once per day.

Stimulant Medications

Stimulants are the most well-known kind of drug recommended for attention deficit disorder. They have the longest reputation for treating ADHD and the most research to go down their effectiveness. The stimulant class of prescription incorporates broadly utilized medications, for example, **Ritalin, Adderall, and Dexedrine.**

<u>Stimulants are accepted to work by increasing dopamine levels in the cerebrum.</u> Dopamine is a neurotransmitter connected with inspiration, delight, attention, and development. For some individuals with ADHD, stimulant medications boost concentration and center while lessening hyperactive and indiscreet practices.

Stimulants for ADHD come in both short-and long-acting measurements. Short-acting stimulants top following a few hours, and must be taken 2-3 times each day. Long-acting or amplified discharge stimulants last 8-12 hours, and are generally taken just once every day.

The long-acting forms of ADHD drug are frequently favored, since individuals with ADHD regularly experience difficulty recollecting taking their pills. Taking only one dose a day is much less demanding and more helpful.

Common side effects of stimulants for ADD / ADHD:

- Feeling restless and jittery
- Difficulty sleeping
- Loss of appetite
- Headaches
- Upset stomach
- Irritability, mood swings
- Depression
- Dizziness
- Racing heartbeat
- Tics

Stimulant medications might likewise bring about identity changes. A few individuals get to be pulled back, drowsy, inflexible, or less unconstrained and chatty. Others create over the top habitual side effects. Since stimulants raise circulatory strain and heart rate, numerous specialists stress over the threats of taking these ADHD drugs for amplified periods.

Safety Concerns

Past the potential side effects, there is various security concerns connected with the stimulant medications for ADHD.

Impact on the creating mind – The long haul effect of ADHD pharmaceutical on the young, creating cerebrum is not yet known. A few scientists are worried that the utilization of medications, for example, Ritalin in kids and youngsters may meddle with ordinary mental health.

Heart-related issues – ADHD stimulant medications have been found to bring about sudden passing in kids and grown-ups with heart conditions. The American Heart Association suggests that all people, including youngsters, have a cardiovascular assessment before beginning a stimulant. An electrocardiogram is suggested if the individual has a background marked by heart issues.

Psychiatric issues – Stimulants for ADHD can trigger or compound side effects of threatening vibe, animosity, nervousness, sadness, and suspicion. Individuals with an individual or family history of suicide, melancholy, or bipolar disorder are at an especially high hazard, and ought to be deliberately monitored while taking stimulants.

Potential for misuse – Stimulant misuse is a developing issue, especially among high school students and youthful grown-ups. Undergrads take them for a boost when packing for exams or pulling dusk 'til dawn affairs. Others misuse stimulant meds for their weight reduction properties. On the off chance that your child is taking stimulants, ensure he or she isn't sharing the pills or selling them to others.

Most Common ADHD drugs

Here is a list of the most commonly prescribed ADHD drugs and information about each one:

Ritalin, Mehylin, Metadate, Concerta, Daytrana (methylphenidate)

This stimulant can effectively deal with the majority of the essential side effects of ADHD —impulsivity, hyperactivity, and inattention. Concentrates on demonstrate that methylphenidate offers the most huge and snappy diminishment of ADHD side effects and doesn't expand tics. Potential side effects incorporate gloom, tipsiness, cerebral pains, craving misfortune, sleep deprivation, and sickness. Considers have demonstrated that **Ritalin** may negatively affect the solid advancement of the cerebrum in kids and adolescents. **Concerta** is a developed discharge type of methylphenidate. **Daytrana** contains the same prescription in a patch that is connected to the skin day by day.

Adderall (dextroamphetamine and amphetamine)

This stimulant can effectively deal with the greater part of the essential indications of ADHD, with all the potential side effects of Ritalin. Concentrates on have demonstrated an uncommon side impact of heart assaults, which can be deadly, especially if blended with liquor use.

Dexedrine (dextroamphetamine)
This stimulant can effectively deal with the greater part of the essential manifestations of ADHD, with all the potential side effects of different stimulants. Examines demonstrate some proof that **dextroamphetamine** might build tics after drawn out stretches of time when given in more noteworthy than-ordinary doses and ought not be regulated at such levels.

Vyvanse (lisdexamfetamine dimesylate)
This stimulant is known as a pro-drug, which means it is idle until metabolized in the body. **Vyvanse** might keep the potential for medication manhandle that has been accounted for with Adderall.

Focalin (dexmethylphenidate)
This stimulant arrives in a container, which can be opened and sprinkled on nourishments for the individuals who experience difficulty gulping pills. Despite the fact that it is known not less side effects than Ritalin, this medication might quit working sooner than required in a few people.

Aplezin, Wellbutrin, Zyban (buproprion)
This stimulant influences the chemicals dopamine and norepinephrine in the cerebrum and can be an extremely effective treatment in individuals who have both ADHD

and sadness. **Buproprion** can effectively oversee side effects of hyperactivity and inattention in individuals who don't discover help from stimulants or who can't endure their side effects. However, antidepressants have not been observed to be effective at overseeing impulsivity. Side effects can incorporate hazy vision, tiredness, dryness of the mouth, and obstruction. Considers have demonstrated that a few antidepressants can expand the danger of suicide. Antidepressants are not affirmed by the U.S. Nourishment and Drug Administration (FDA) for the treatment of ADHD.

Intuniv, Tenex (guanfacine)

Intuniv, a long-acting type of the circulatory strain pharmaceutical **Tenex**, was endorsed for the treatment of ADHD by the FDA in September 2009. This once-a-day treatment for children ages 6 to 17 is a non-stimulant prescription thought to draw in receptors in the territory of the mind connected to ADHD. In 2011, the FDA said that **Intuniv** could be utilized alongside a stimulant to help youngsters who are not reacting great to a stimulant alone. **Guanfacine** can fortify memory, lessen diversion, and enhance attention and drive control. Side effects can incorporate tiredness, stomach torment, discombobulating, a drop in pulse, dry mouth, and obstruction.

Catapres (clonidine)

This hypertension solution can oversee ADHD indications of forceful conduct, impulsions, hyperactivity, and tics, yet it's not extremely effective against inattention. Side effects can incorporate languor, dryness of the mouth, hazy vision, heart issues, and obstruction. Thinks about have demonstrated this hypertension solution is turning out to be more prominent and is a sheltered and fruitful treatment for ADHD notwithstanding or rather than stimulant medications, however it is not FDA-endorsed for this utilization.

Strattera

Strattera, likewise known by its generic name **atomoxetine**, is the main non-stimulant drug affirmed by the FDA for ADD/ADHD treatment. Not at all like stimulants, which influence dopamine, **Strattera** boosts the levels of norepinephrine, an alternate cerebrum compound.

Strattera is longer-acting than the stimulant medications. Its effects last more than 24 hours production it a decent alternative for the individuals who experience difficulty getting going in the morning. Since it has some upper properties, it's additionally a top decision for those with coinciding tension or wretchedness. Another in addition to is that it doesn't fuel tics or **Tourette's Syndrome.**

<u>Then again, Strattera doesn't seem, by all accounts, to be as effective as the stimulant medications for treating indications of hyperactivity.</u>

Common side effects of Strattera include:

- Sleepiness
- Headache
- Abdominal pain or upset stomach

- Nausea and vomiting
- Dizziness
- Mood swings
- Sleepiness
- Headache
- Abdominal pain or upset stomach
- Nausea and vomiting
- Dizziness
- Mood swings

With patience and a knowledgeable medical professional, you can find the right medication at the right dose to help manage ADHD symptoms.

Chapter 6: Non-Medical Treatment

There are numerous protected, effective medications that can help and treatment meanwhile doesn't as a matter of course mean pills or doctors' workplaces. Any move you make to deal with your side effects can be considered treatment. Keeping in mind you might need to look for expert help along the way; at last, you are the one in control. You don't need to sit tight for a determination or depend on experts. There's a great deal you can do to help yourself.

When you consider treatment for ADHD, do you instantly hop to **Ritalin**? Numerous individuals liken ADHD treatment with medicine. In any case, comprehend that solution for ADHD doesn't work for everybody, and notwithstanding when it works, it won't tackle all issues or totally wipe out side effects.

Truth be told, while drug for ADHD regularly enhances attention and concentration, it ordinarily does almost no to help side effects of complication, poor time administration, absent mindedness, and tarrying the very issues that cause the most issues for some grown-ups with ADHD.

Exercise

Exercising routinely is one of the least demanding and best approaches to decrease the side effects of ADHD and enhance concentration, inspiration, memory, and state of mind.

Physical movement quickly boosts the cerebrum's dopamine, norepinephrine, and serotonin levels all of which influence center and attention. Thusly, exercise and medications for ADHD, for example, Ritalin and Adderall work comparably. Be that as it may, dissimilar to ADHD medicine, exercise doesn't require a remedy and its side impact free.

- **Attempt to exercise on most days -** You don't need to go to the rec center. A 30-minute walk four times each week is sufficient to give advantages. Thirty minutes of movement consistently is stunningly better.
- **Pick something pleasant, so you'll stay with it -** Pick exercises that play to your physical qualities or that you find testing yet fun. Group activities can be a decent decision in light of the fact that the social component keeps them intriguing.
- **Get out into nature -** Thinks about demonstrate that investing energy in nature can diminish the manifestations of ADHD. Get serious about the advantages by joining "green time" with exercise. Take a stab at trekking, trail running, or strolling in a neighborhood park or grand territory.

Sleep
Numerous grown-ups with ADHD have sleep troubles. The most well-known issues include:

- Trouble getting to sleep at night, often because racing thoughts is keeping you up.
- **Restless sleep** - You may toss and turn throughout the night, tear the covers apart, and wake up at any little noise.
- **Trouble getting up in the morning** - Awakening is an everyday battle. You might rest through various alerts and feel sleepy and fractious for quite a long time subsequent to getting up.

Low quality sleep makes the side effects of ADHD more terrible, so getting on a normal rest timetable is vital. Enhancing the nature of your rest can have a major effect in your attention, center, and mind-set.

Relaxation techniques
A number of the side effects of ADHD can be alleviated by unwinding procedures, for example, contemplation and yoga. At the point when drilled reliably, these quieting treatments work to expand attention and center and diminish impulsivity, uneasiness, and melancholy.

Meditation
Meditation is a type of centered examination that unwinds the brain and the body and focuses your contemplations.

Scientists say that over the long haul, meditation expands movement in the prefrontal cortex, the part of the cerebrum in charge of attention, arranging, and motivation control.

As it were, meditation is the inverse of ADHD. The objective of meditation is to prepare yourself to center your attention with the objective of accomplishing knowledge. So it's a workout for your attention compass that additionally may offer you some assistance with understanding and work out issues.

Professional Therapy

Treatment for ADHD can likewise mean looking for outside help. Experts prepared in ADHD can offer you some assistance with learning new abilities to adapt to side effects and change propensities that are bringing about issues.

A few treatments concentrate on overseeing push and outrage or controlling hasty practices, while others show you how to handle time and cash better and enhance your hierarchical abilities.

Talk treatment
Grown-ups with ADHD regularly battle with issues coming from longstanding examples of underachievement, disappointment, scholastic challenges, work turnover, and relationship struggle. Singular talk treatment can offer you some assistance with dealing with this psychological weight, including low self-regard, the sentiments of humiliation and disgrace you might have encountered as a tyke and young person, and disdain at the pestering and feedback you get from individuals near you.

Marriage and family treatment

Marriage and family treatment addresses the issues ADD/ADHD can make in your connections and family life, for example, clashes over cash issues, overlooked duties, obligations in the home, and incautious decisions. Treatment can help you and your friends and family investigate these issues and concentrate on productive methods for managing them and speaking with one another. Treatment can likewise enhance your connections by instructing your accomplice and relatives about ADHD.

Psychological behavioral treatment

Subjective behavioral treatment urges you to distinguish and change the negative convictions and practices that are bringing about issues throughout your life. Since numerous people with ADHD are crippled from years of battle and unmet desires, one of the fundamental objectives of intellectual behavioral treatment is to change this antagonistic standpoint into a more cheerful, sensible perspective. Subjective behavioral treatment additionally concentrates on the functional issues that frequently accompany ADHD, for example, disruption, work execution issues, and poor time administration.

Professional Organizers

An professional organizer can be exceptionally useful on the off chance that you experience issues sorting out your effects or your time. Coordinators can offer you some assistance with reducing mess, grow better authoritative frameworks, and figure out how to deal with your time proficiently. An expert coordinator goes to your home or working environment, takes a gander at how you have things composed (or not sorted out), and after that recommends changes. Notwithstanding helping you to sort out your research material and bill paying, an expert coordinator has proposals for memory and arranging devices, documenting frameworks, and that's only the tip of the iceberg. An expert coordinator additionally assists with time-administration: your errands, your schedule, and your date-book.

Section C: Fixing ADHD with Diet

Chapter 7: Food Sensitivities of Patients

As of late, a conceivable relationship in the middle of ADHD and food sensitivities is being talked about more because of consequences of broad testing and clinical exploration. The indications of food sensitivities and ADHD are strikingly comparable and bring up the issue of whether a few individuals are being misdiagnosed with ADHD, when they might be having a characteristic response to or even a hypersensitive response to food, food added substances, or colors which is inciting such manifestations.

Food decisions can adversely influence the levels of brain neurotransmitters and hormones, which are imperatively essential in the regulation of mind-set, rest, hankering, attention and drive control. Certain foods are known not to hyperactivity and outrage issues, two signs or indications regularly connected with ADHD.

For quite a long time, doctors have speculated that specific foods might have something to do with ADHD. Although much research has been done on the subject's, despite everything it not trusted that food really causes ADHD. What a few foods do appear to do, however, is intensify ADHD manifestations or influence conduct that emulates the indications of ADHD in kids. Over the top caffeine and unreasonable utilization of quick foods and different foods of poor nourishing worth can make kids show conduct that may be mistaken for ADHD.

Milk and Cheese

Dairy items contain a compound called **casein** which specialists suspect might assume a part in increasing side effects of ADHD because of casein bigotry. In people who can't completely breakdown the proteins in casein, a substance stays in their framework that in the long run produces opium-like indications, for example, the trademark "spaciness" and poor attention compass displayed in those determined to have ADHD. Coincidently, a significant number of individuals experiencing ADHD subsequent to decreasing the measure of dairy items in their eating regimen experienced improved psychological capacities and less "mind mist".

Wheat, Rye and Barley

Gluten-Sensitive Enteropathy, or Celiac malady, is brought on by the protein gluten found in foods containing wheat, rye and grain. When somebody experiences this ailment for quite a long while without an appropriate determination, (as with numerous occasions of ADHD and food sensitivities) harm is done to parts of the digestive system in charge of engrossing fundamental supplements. In this way, the individual can't take in these supplements and experiences numerous manifestations, for example,

- malnourishment
- poor development
- formative deferrals
- stomach illnesses
- bloating

Since the body is not getting the vitamins fundamental to solid improvement, the mind is likewise straightforwardly influenced by this absence of supplements and starts to breakdown. Learning issues and poor attention compass in youngsters start to show in school, bringing about issues seeing someone and advancement of youth self-regard. In a few exploration concentrates on, kids who killed gluten from their eating regimen demonstrated critical change in these zones once thought to be ADHD-related.

Candy

Candy is stacked with sugar and artificial colors, which are a terrible mix with regards to youngsters with ADHD who regularly need to take after an ADHD diet. Both of these regular fixings have been appeared to advance ADHD side effects specifically hyperactivity in studies. With the high substance of sugar and artificial colors, candy is a colossal contributor to ADHD.

Soda
If you have ADHD, consider wiping out soda. (What's more, regardless of the possibility that you don't have ADHD, saying no to soda is a smart thought at any rate.) These sweet beverages frequently have a large number of the same sugars and sweeteners that make confection an awful thought for children on the ADHD diet. Soda likewise has different fixings that intensify ADHD manifestations, for example, high-fructose corn syrup and caffeine. Intemperate sugar and caffeine admission both reason side effects of hyperactivity and simple distractibility.

Frozen Fruits and Vegetables
Despite the fact that fruits and vegetables are solid decisions for an ADHD eating routine, some frozen assortments can contain counterfeit hues, so check all names deliberately. Frozen foods can fuel ADHD side effects for another reason. Foods treated with organophosphates for bug control have been appeared to bring about neurologic-based behavioral issues that copy ADHD and numerous other conduct issues.

Energy Drinks
Energy drinks are turning out to be increasingly prominent among children, particularly adolescents. Sadly, they additionally have a veritable fortune trove of fixings that can compound ADHD side effects: sugar, fake sweeteners,

counterfeit hues, caffeine, and different stimulants. Energy drinks are high on the rundown of things that make adolescents show practices mirroring ADHD.

Seafood

Eating fish and other seafood with follow measures of **mercury** can intensify ADHD side effects in the long haul. A portion of the most exceedingly terrible offenders are shark, ruler mackerel, swordfish, and tilefish. Mercury, similar to cellulose, is to a great degree difficult to process and can aggregate in the mind after some time. This can prompt hyperactivity. Talk with your doctor or ADHD nutritionist about the best sorts of fish to incorporate into your ADHD diet.

Food Allergies in General

Hypersensitive responses to food can be brought on by any sort of food, yet a few foods are all the more normally found in instances of extreme food sensitivity. A tie in the middle of ADHD and food sensitivities is unquestionably something to consider as a result of those physical indications seen in both ADHD and food hypersensitivities.

Youngsters with learning-behavioral issues frequently have chronic sinus, hacking and ear issues, both of which can be side effects of continuous food hypersensitivities. Rising up out of these wellbeing issues are school-related issues which start influencing kids with ADHD when they start kindergarten. Fretfulness, hostility, distractibility and evident lethargy are characteristics ascribed to a youngster without instructors or folks who comprehend the underlying driver of these issues. <u>A few different side effects that are not generally joined with ADHD food hypersensitivities are:</u>

- halitosis
- headaches
- bed-wetting
- seizures

Chapter 8: The Essential Minerals

ADHD includes neurotransmitter irregular characteristics. Regularly, individuals with ADHD additionally have inadequacies or awkward nature in basic supplements that are utilized to make these neurotransmitters in the body. On the off chance that we test understanding with ADHD, we frequently see that they are not exceptionally effective at processing and using their food, and might even have parasites, candida or different indications of more genuine gut awkward nature.

Supporting the nourishing needs of a patient with ADHD can truly help instructive and conduct mediations "stick". Solid nutritional support for ADHD incorporates support for the cerebrum, gut and digestion system.

Most ADHD professionals recommend eating a diet full of fruits and vegetables, complex carbs, and some lean protein with every meal to help manage symptoms. However, not everyone eats the right foods to achieve beneficial levels of certain nutrients. In other cases, our bodies don't produce some nutrients we need, so we have to get them from supplements. It has been found that there are essential vitamins and minerals for managing ADHD.

Magnesium

Magnesium is extremely quieting, and has been known as the "counter push" mineral. Low magnesium and stress fortify one another: Stress of any sort brings down magnesium levels, and low magnesium levels increment weight on the body. In studies, kids with ADHD who were insufficient in magnesium demonstrated noteworthy change in hyperactivity in the wake of taking magnesium supplements.

Magnesium is fundamental for energy generation, cell replication and uprightness, detoxification, glutathione union, solid/neurological capacity, and keeping up body pH equalization.

Magnesium insufficiency has long been thought to assume a significant role in the auditory sensitivity or insensitivity common with patient with ADHD. This might happen with a transcendence of calcium that can make a magnesium lack, encouraging an expanded arrival of glutamate, and bringing about an over-incitement of the sound-related nerve.

<u>One incredible approach to add additional magnesium to your life is to add a measure of quieting Epsom salts to shower, as a tender approach to begin backing off for sleep time around evening time. Epsom salts (Magnesium Sulfate) are protected and non-dangerous.</u>

Zinc

Zinc is a critical element in the metabolism of neurotransmitters, prostaglandins, and for keeping up cerebrum structure and work. Numerous studies have demonstrated that zinc supplementation is useful with memory, speculation and I.Q. Dopamine is a standout amongst the most essential elements in the pathophysiology of hyperactivity disorder, and the hormone melatonin has a critical part in the regulation of dopamine. Since zinc is vital in the digestion system of melatonin, it bodes well that zinc is a vital component in the treatment of attention deficit and hyperactivity disorder (ADHD). **Clams are an especially rich food wellspring of zinc.**

Researchers have demonstrated behavioral upgrades in light of zinc supplementation. In one six-week twofold visually impaired and placebo treatment controlled study, kids taking 15mg of zinc sulfate + methylphenidate scored fundamentally higher on a Parent and Teacher Rating Scale than those taking methylphenidate alone. <u>Another study demonstrated critical behavioral change when kids were given supplemental zinc, magnesium and calcium.</u>

Selenium

Despite the fact that there is minimal direct confirmation to bolster the case, a few specialists have expressed that selenium could treat ADHD. This case depends on the conviction that a lot of the substantial metal mercury in the body could prompt ADHD.

Scientific exploration has demonstrated that selenium helps reduce the lethal effects of mercury particularly its most naturally harming structure, methyl mercury. It does as such by "recovering" certain regular cell reinforcements in the body that work to evacuate methyl mercury. However, more research should be ruined this treatment strategy to be broadly acknowledged.

Fish Oil

Essential Fatty Acids (EFAs) help with brain and nerve advancement, cell correspondence, oxygenation, metabolism and safe reaction.

<u>In individuals with ADHD, Omega-3 EFAs, for example, DHA and EPA are especially imperative for the mind, the invulnerable framework, and to battle irritation.</u>

Numerous studies demonstrate that EFA supplementation can likewise help with positive state of mind and attention. EFAs are considered "essential" since they are required all through the human life cycle, can't be delivered in the human body, and accordingly should be given through the eating regimen.

Probiotics

Not at all like in Autism, most people with ADHD do not show gut symptoms. The vast majority with ADHD have minimal great microscopic organisms and high measures of destructive microbes in their stomach. <u>Adding probiotics to the eating regimens of people with ADHD, the possibly unsafe microscopic organisms will diminish and the side effects of ADHD will likewise be decreased.</u>

Consequently, it bodes well to incorporate a decent wide range probiotic in the supplement regimen of any individual with ADHD. Anyone with ADHD who enhances while beginning probiotics, or demonstrates gastrointestinal side effects, for example, looseness of the bowels, stoppage, bloating or gas ought to be tried for parasites and other intestinal issues, and might profit by the utilization of a more exceptional probiotic.

L-Carnitine

L-carnitine is delivered from an amino acid and it helps body cells produce energy. <u>A study including a gathering of young men with ADHD found that 54% of them indicated improvement in conduct while taking L-carnitine.</u>

L-carnitine has not been examined for wellbeing in kids, so converse with your social insurance specialist before giving L-carnitine to a kid.

If you are searching for protected and option treatment for ADHD, then consider utilizing **Listol** which contains these fixings: Vitamin B6, Iron, Magnesium, and Zinc.

ADHD Specific Supplements

There are a few supplements that are made in light of the ADHD patient. These for the most part contain a blend of essential vitamins and minerals alongside different fixings that have been appeared to help with manifestations, for example, grape seed separate. Once in a while they incorporate essential fatty acids in addition to other things. Here's a gander at a couple of well-known offering ADHD supplements:

- **BioFocus Bars** are intended for a between supper nibble or feast substitution. <u>It helps in adjusting glucose levels, enhancing supplement thickness, and supporting neurological and intellectual capacity</u>. They are made with natural fixings and chocolate nutty spread crunch seasoned.
- **Learner's Edge by Integrative Therapeautics** is made to bolster neurological improvement and capacity in youngsters. **It contains DMAE (**a substance that has been appeared to improve mental concentration and intellectual capacity), **Acetyl L-carnitine** to cushion oxidative anxiety, **L-theanine** to bolster neurotransmitter action and **Carnosine** to bolster sound frontal projection movement.
- **Dynamic Kids Drink** is an organic product punch enhanced hotspot for characteristic vitamins, minerals, cell reinforcements and essential fatty acids Omega 6 and 9 found in the Acai Berry. This beverage was really made by a mother who needed her kids to get the best possible measures of supplements. Keeping up a sound eating routine including fruits and vegetables can be testing with regards to our youngsters! The following is an audit from a mother, and client of Natural Healthy Concepts, who felt it had a tremendous effect with her kid.

Chapter 9: Omega-3 Fatty Acids

EPA, or eicosapentaenoic acid, and DHA, or docosahexaenoic acid, are omega-3 fatty acids in fish oil. Specialists reporting issue of "Prostaglandins, Leukotrienes and Essential Fatty Acids" portray omega-3s as essential both for solid mental health and upkeep. In spite of the fact that ADHD is normally connected with youth conducts disorders, a couple researches have taken a gander at advantages of supplementing omega-3s in grown-ups with ADHD.

What are Omega-3 Fatty Acids?

Omega-3 fatty acids (ALA, EPA, and DHA) are critical supplements. There is an abundance of information in the medical writing about the cardiovascular advantages of omega-3 supplements. Omega-3 supplements have been appeared to lessen the danger of sudden cardiovascular demise and heart assault, moderate development of plaque in the courses by diminishing irritation, enhance lipid levels, upgrade circulatory strain regulation, and decrease beat pressure. <u>Because of these advantages, scientists suggests eating 2 servings of fatty fish week by week.</u>

Omega-3 in Adult ADHD

By, an association dedicated to serving kids and grown-ups with ADHD, numerous grown-ups live with indications for a considerable length of time before being analyzed, which makes one wonder of what number of stay undiscovered. Roughly 60 percent of youngsters with ADHD experience side effects into adulthood. Around 4 percent of grown-up Americans are in no time determined to have ADHD. Determined underachievement, wastefulness, absent mindedness and chronic self-belittlement are basic manifestations. If you have these side effects, a qualified proficient can figure out whether these issues are a direct result of ADHD.

Why Should You Opt for Omega-3?

Omega-3s have been examined for ADHD advantages in view of the way of the disorder. In ADHD, cerebrum science is defective because of the disappointment of neurotransmitters to transfer signals between nerve cells. Neurotransmitters are mind chemicals, and dopamine is the neurotransmitter in charge of concentration. The fundamental auxiliary segments of nerve cells are omega-3 fatty acids. In ADHD, the nerve cells are omega-3 inadequate, hindering dopamine's transmission from nerve cell to nerve cell. ADHD medications cause dopamine to be pushed over the cells, so center is made strides. Researchers have wanted to accomplish comparable advantages from omega-3 supplementation.

Omega-3 vs. Omega-6 fatty acids

At the onset of the industrial upset (around 140 years prior), there was a stamped shift in the ratio of n-6 to n-3 fatty acids in the eating routine. Utilization of n-6 fats expanded to the detriment of n-3 fats. This change was because of both the approach of the cutting edge vegetable oil industry and the expanded utilization of oat grains as feed for household animals (which thusly modified the fatty acid profile of meat that people devoured).

Ratio of Omega-6 to Omega-3
Vegetable oil utilization climbed significantly between the starting and end of the twentieth century, and this had a completely unsurprising impact on the ratio of omega-6 to omega-3 fats. As this ratio was 8:1 during those times but later with research and development in health industries, it was found out that omega-6 fatty acids have a marked damaging effect on health. **Today, the ratio between omega-6 and omega-3 is 16:1 in normal diet.** This is the main reason for the cause of ADHD in children as well as some adults as EPD and DHA which are primarily present in Omega-3 fatty acids (good fatty acids) are taken low in diet and these prevent ADHD by improving behavior and concentration in children.

Omega-6 and Omega-3 fatty acids compete
You should know that n-6 and n-3 fatty acids compete for the same conversion enzymes. This implies the amount of n-6 in the eating routine straightforwardly influences the conversion of n-3 ALA, found in plant foods, to long-chain n-3 EPA and DHA, which shield us from ailment.

A few studies have demonstrated that the biological accessibility and action of n-6 fatty acids are contrarily identified with the concentration of n-3 fatty acids in tissue. Studies have likewise demonstrated that more prominent creation of EPA and DHA in layers decreases the accessibility of AA for eicosanoid production.

Effect of Omega-6 on ADHD

Since people intake more omega-6 than omega-3 fatty acids, hence there is a greater concentration of n-6 in the body tissues as compared to n-3. The greater availability of n-6 to the tissues causes inflammation in the tissue and causes great damage to the normal functionality of the tissues. What this means is that the more omega-3 fat you eat, the less omega-6 will be available to the tissues to produce inflammation. <u>Omega-6 is pro-inflammatory, while omega-3 is neutral</u>. **A diet with a lot of omega-6 and not much omega-3 will increase inflammation. A diet of a lot of omega-3 and not much omega-6 will reduce inflammation.**

Now as inflammation increase and there is less availability of EPA and DHA for brain to function properly as compared to omega-6 supplements, the normal behavior of brain is damaged which causes the biggest problem for ADHD patients especially those who are in starting stage of ADHD development. This could worsen the situation for them.

Fish for Omega-3?

Fish is an unfavorable wellspring of omega-3s on the grounds that most fatty fish contain hurtful contamination, for example, dioxin and mercury. Individuals likewise report difficulty processing fish oils as a result of the fishy taste and rancidity. Purified fish oils are an alternative; however the expanded interest for fish and fish oils is draining our seas of fish.

Additionally, since pregnant ladies are encouraged to point of confinement fish admission (to keep away from the potential mischief of mercury to the patient's mind), supplemental omega-3 fatty acids are a more secure option.

Scientific Dosage
Scientists depicted clinical trials analyzing the effects of omega-3s on ADHD side effects. Although most studies had been performed on kids, the specialists portrayed one study in which a gathering of 36 grown-up patients with both ADHD and sadness were supplemented 3,000 mg of DHA every day for three months. Toward the end of the trial, members' obliviousness score tumbled from a normal of 94 toward the begin of the trial to 17 percent toward the end

Dosage for Adults
To treat attention-deficit hyperactivity disorder (ADHD) in adults, 210 milligrams of omega-3 fatty acids has been taken by mouth for seven weeks. Doses of 160 to 2000 milligrams of EPA plus 4 to 858 milligrams of DHA have been taken by mouth daily for up to 32 weeks.

Dosage for Children

To treat attention-deficit hyperactivity disorder (ADHD), 120 milligrams of ALA has been taken by mouth for seven weeks. Doses of 80-1,000 milligrams of EPA plus 2.7-558 milligrams of DHA have been taken by mouth daily for up to 30 weeks.

Chapter 10: Foods to Avoid

Many experts believe eating particular foods can trigger ADHD symptoms in patients, particularly children, so it's important to avoid certain foods thought to spark a reaction.

If you or someone you love suffers from ADHD, try avoiding these foods. Eliminating (or strongly reducing) these foods from your diet can help manage the symptoms of ADHD.

Ice Cream

Dairy items, for example, ice cream, can trigger ADHD in Individuals why should excessively touchy milk items. Somebody who is touchy to dairy items might feel tired both physically and rationally subsequent to expending foods, for example, dessert. Thus, it's best to maintain a strategic distance from this cool treat – despite the fact that it might appear like a smart thought at the time.

Coffee

This might be a difficult one for some people to surrender, considering espresso is such a prevalent beverage. Numerous individuals depend on espresso for a fiery begins to their mornings. Shockingly, espresso contains a significant measure of caffeine which – a characteristic stimulant known not ADHD side effects. If your indications deteriorate in the wake of drinking espresso, you can take a stab at drinking natural teas or decaffeinated espresso instead.

Swordfish

Fish high in mercury, for example, swordfish, have been known not ADHD manifestations. The overwhelming metal (mercury) found in this sort of fish can diminishing one's capacity to center and impedes concentration in numerous people. If you see your side effects deteriorating in the wake of eating this kind of fish, select fish with lower mercury levels, for example, shrimp, lobster or salmon.

Chocolate

Chocolate, similar to espresso, contains a significant measure of caffeine. Caffeine has been known not ADHD indications and can exacerbate side effects if you pick not to dispose of it from your eating routine. If you see your indications turn out to be more awful in the wake of eating chocolate or drinking hot chocolate, you might need to settle on white chocolate items.

Frozen Pizza

Frozen pizzas are pressed brimming with artificial hues and flavorings, much the same as pop. The fixings used to upgrade these sorts of items can expand hyperactivity and diminish concentration in people with this disorder. If you like eating pizza, consider making one sans preparation all alone. Along these lines, you'll know the majority of the fixings utilized are solid and regular.

Corn

Yellow vegetables, for example, corn, are known not responses in people with ADHD. It is suggested that you avoid eating these sorts of vegetables keeping in mind the end goal to control your indications. If you need to eat wellbeing, decide on different vegetables such as spinach, peppers or tomatoes.

Chips

It's essentially a given that chips would be on this rundown. Actually, most garbage foods ought to be kept away from so as to deal with this sort of disorder. Chips are likewise high in artificial hues and enhancing, settling on them a poor decision for people searching for an ADHD cordial eating regimen. If you like eating, consider eating solid vegetables to control your hankering, rather than garbage foods like chips and chocolate.

Squash

Squash is another yellow food to dodge when managing ADHD. For the same reasons as corn, squash has been known not flare ups. Not every single yellow food is terrible for ADHD sufferers – bananas are alright in light of the fact that the genuine banana is white. Just the peel of the bananas is yellow, and you don't eat the yellow part at any rate. As we said before, select solid (conceivably natural) vegetables rather than yellow one

Red Meat

Red meat has been known not an expansion of manifestations for ADHD sufferers, specialists say. Decreasing your red meat admission (not as a matter of course dispensing with it totally) might demonstrate awesome advantages with regards to controlling your ADHD. As said before, deciding on more advantageous choices such as salmon or shrimp will keep your manifestations controlled so you can keep up a more beneficial, more satisfied life.

Cheese

Another dairy food to maintain a strategic distance from when attempting to abstain from starting ADHD indications is cheddar (specifically bovine's cheddar). Much like yogurt and dessert, wiping out cheddar from your eating regimen for six to eight weeks will figure out if it's the reason for your flare-ups. If you see your manifestations are more controllable when you're not eating cheddar (or other cow dairy items), consider changing to a without lactose or bovine dairy free eating regimen (i.e., eat goat's cheddar).

Section D: What to Eat?

Chapter 11: ADHD Diet and Nutritional Supplements

It might incorporate the foods you eat and any nutritious supplements you might take. Ideally, you're dietary patterns would offer the cerebrum some assistance with working better and diminish side effects, for example, fretfulness or absence of core interest. You might catch wind of these decisions that you could concentrate on:

General nourishment: The presumption is that a few foods you eat might exacerbate your indications better or. You may likewise not be eating a few things that could improve side effects.

Supplementation diet: With this arrangement you include vitamins, minerals, or different supplements. The thought is that it could offer you some assistance with making up for not getting enough of these through what you eat. Supporters of these weight control plans surmise that if you don't get enough of specific supplements, it might add to your indications.

Disposal counts calories: These include not eating foods or ingredients that you think may be setting off specific practices or aggravating your side effects.

Nutrition from Foods

Numerous wellbeing specialists imagine that what you eat and drink might assume a part in helping manifestations.

Specialists say that whatever is useful for the cerebrum is prone to be useful for ADHD. You might need to eat:

A high-protein diet
Beans, cheddar, eggs, meat, and nuts can be great wellsprings of protein. Eat these sorts of foods in the morning and for after-school snacks. It might enhance concentration and perhaps make ADHD medications work for more.

Less basic sugars
Eliminated what number of these you eat: confection, corn syrup, nectar, sugar, items produced using white flour, white rice, and potatoes without the skins.

More unpredictable carbs
These are the great folks. Load up on vegetables and a few fruits, including oranges, tangerines, pears, grapefruit, apples, and kiwi. Eat this kind of food at night and it might offer you some assistance with sleeping.

More omega-3 fatty acids
You can discover these in fish, salmon, and other chilly water white fish. Walnuts, Brazil nuts, and olive and canola oil are different foods with these in them. You could likewise take an omega-3 fatty acid supplement.

Best Foods for ADHD

Before we get to the rundown of foods you ought to (and ought not) eat, we have to stretch this: Every patient is different and will respond to specific foods differently. A few individuals have unfavorably susceptible responses to specific sorts of food (dairy and so forth.) which can trigger ADHD indications. It's generally best to converse with your doctor before rolling out any significant improvements to slim down.

That being said, there are certain types of foods that have been known to either help or hurt your suffering from ADHD. Foods that contain artificial sweeteners, foods that contain high measures of sugar, immersed fat or caffeine and handled foods like store meat have been connected to activating ADHD side effects in individuals. Then again, foods high in Vitamin B, protein, calcium and follow minerals have the inverse impact on patient and can really reduce manifestations all the time.

Apples

Apples are an extraordinary wellspring of complex sugars. Doctors have suggested that youngsters with ADHD expand their admission of complex sugars. Eating these sorts of foods just before bed has additionally been known not youngsters rest better. An apple a day will keep your ADHD indications under control.

Goat's Cheese

Cheese is an extraordinary wellspring of protein and protein. However, numerous who experience the ill effects of ADHD endure with a dairy animals' milk hypersensitivity or bigotry, which can worsen ADHD manifestations. If you think your kid has sensitivity to bovine's milk/dairy, have a go at changing to goat cheddar rather to enhance concentration and enhance how ADHD prescription functions.

Pears

Much like apples, pears are a decent wellspring of complex sugars. If your kid doesn't care for apples (or you're simply hoping to change up their eating routine), pears are an incredible option. Like apples and other complex carbs, eating pears around evening time can help rest.

Eggs

Eggs are additionally an extraordinary wellspring of protein. Protein is essential in keeping up adjusted eating routine and controlling manifestations in kids with ADHD. Much like cheddar, eggs will enhance concentration and build the time ADHD medications work. Eggs (particularly hard boiled since you can make them early and have them close by) are an extraordinary breakfast alternative for guardian.

Nuts
Like fish, nuts are an extraordinary wellspring of **Omega-3 fatty acids**. Walnuts and Brazil nuts have been appeared to have the most effect while overseeing ADHD manifestations yet different sorts like almonds are an extraordinary option too.

Spinach
Spinach is a standout amongst the best vegetables with regards to controlling ADHD manifestations in youngsters. Doctors frequently suggest verdant green vegetables and spinach is without a doubt at the highest priority on that rundown. There are numerous approaches to add spinach to your eating routine. If your tyke declines to eat it, mix it up alongside berries and different fruits in a smoothie and they'll never at any point know they're eating it.

Kiwi
Kids love kiwis! Much like oranges, apples and pears, kiwis are an incredible wellspring of complex sugars. This natural product is heavenly and amusing to eat as well as it's an incredible option for folks hoping to change up their kids' eating methodologies. Eating apples and pears ordinary can get exhausting. Including some kiwi will put a grin on your children's countenances and will guarantee they're eating great as well!

Whole Grain Cereals

Grain can be an extremely solid breakfast choice for children experiencing ADHD however there are a couple key things to recall. To begin with, you'll generally need to pick multi-grain alternatives. Rather than typical Cheerios, pick multigrain. Also, you'll need to maintain a strategic distance from grains with artificial hues and artificial sweeteners. What does that mean? It essentially implies pick sorts like Corn Flakes and Fiber 1 rather than Fruit Loops and Lucky Charms.

Chapter 12: Vitamins

Nutritional deficiencies contribute unequivocally to the indications of ADHD. While the individuals from the Vitamin B complex are the most widely recognized vitamins endorsed for supplementation in individuals determined to have ADHD, different vitamins have auxiliary parts in the advancement and treatment of this hyperactivity disorder.

The B vitamins are critical in ADHD treatment for two noteworthy reasons. To start with, some of them, particularly Vitamin B6 and B12, are essential for the advancement of the sensory system and the union of neurotransmitters.

Also, these B vitamins are required for the regulation of sugar metabolism. Such regulation is critical to adjust the glucose level in the blood.

Since sugary foods surge the body with glucose and cause hyperactivity all the while, these vitamins direct the arrival of glucose and give a more adjusted energy supply.

Vitamin B6

Vitamin B6 or Pyridoxine is vital for the two reasons given above: it is essential for the regulation of sugar (and even protein) metabolism; and it adds to parts of mind science and focal sensory system.

Vitamin B6 is likewise required in the body for the generation of specific neurotransmitters, for example, dopamine, serotonin and norepinephrine.

Indications of Vitamin B6 deficiency incorporate irritability, limited capacity to focus and transient memory misfortune. Supplementation for kids determined to have ADHD is prompted. <u>Day by day doses of Vitamin B6 suggested for ADHD is 25-50 mg albeit high doses have been accounted for as effective.</u>

Vitamin B6 is actually found in chestnut rice, vegetables, entire grains and meats.

Vitamin B12

Vitamin B12 or **Cyanocobalamin** is expected to bolster ideal neurological capacities. Vitamin B12 deficiency delivers some ADHD-like side effects, for example, perplexity and memory misfortune.

Supplementation with the vitamin enhances center and attention in kids determined to have ADHD. Alongside Vitamin B6 and B9, **cyanocobalamin** is required in the body for combining and directing neurotransmitters.

Vitamin B3

Vitamin B3 might reduce the seriousness of behavioral issues, loss of psychological capacity and hyperactivity that regularly go with ADHD. This vitamin additionally quiets your sensory system, so it might control eagerness and touchiness. Vitamin B3 assists with conveyance of magnesium, vitamin C, zinc and calcium to the mind.

Other B Vitamins

Other B vitamins helpful for treating ADHD incorporate those required for keeping up general wellbeing. These incorporate Vitamin B1 which is helpful in the change of starches to glucose. Vitamin B2 is additionally required for this reason.

<u>Vitamin B3 or niacin is imperative for general metabolism and to enhance the ingestion of essential minerals and vitamins from the gastrointestinal tract.</u>

Vitamins A and E

In spite of the fact that Vitamin A and E are for the most part not prescribed for any capacity to enhance mind capacity, they individuals living with ADHD in different ways.

For instance, these vitamins are required for enhancing vision. Meandering center and mindlessness in ADHD youngsters, particularly in the classroom, are in some cases because of the way that their visual perceptions are sufficiently bad to connect with perusing materials or see writing slates.

Vitamin A is the most critical regular supplement for sound vision. It limits to the poles and cones of the eyes where it is in charge of catching light and activating signs in the optic nerve.

Vitamin E is additionally imperative for eye wellbeing. Its deficiency can prompt retinopathy, an eye sickness.

Both Vitamins A and E are likewise cell reinforcements. Thusly, they are essential for cleaning up destructive free radicals in the body. Along these lines, they are additionally defensive and can avert auxiliary harms in the neurons of the focal sensory system.

<u>Fish oil and cod liver oil, which are basic supplements prescribed for treating ADHD, contain these two vitamins.</u>

Vitamin D

Dissimilar to alternate vitamins treated in this article, the connection between Vitamin D and ADHD is not surely known. However, the vitamin is essential in certain key body forms which might add to the result of ADHD.

To start with, Vitamin D is known not the concentration of glutathione in the cerebrum. Glutathione is cell reinforcement helpful for neutralizing unsafe free radicals in the focal sensory system. Its defensive activity averts harm to the neurons and helps in keeping up cerebrum wellbeing.

Also, Vitamin D is required for specific strides in the creations of cerebrum chemicals, for example, dopamine and norepinephrine. The parts of these two neurotransmitters are as of now settled in the improvement and treatment of ADHD.

Also, Vitamin D improves the action of the chemical, choline acetyltransferase. This is the catalyst in charge of the last stride in the result of acetylcholine, the boss cerebrum concoction of the cholinergic branch of the sensory system.

Acetylcholine is known not and expand attention compass, and its concentration in the cerebrum is straightforwardly associated with the capacity to center for managed timeframes.

Section E: Conclusion

ADHD is one of the most common neuropsychological disorder in the modern era especially among the children. The disorder is chronic and appears in as many 60% to 70% of adults who were diagnosed with the condition as children. Symptoms of ADHD disorder include inattention, distractibility, and impulsivity, which are frequently accompanied by physical or motor hyperactivity. Therapy for the condition includes ADHD medications with social, psychological, and behavioral therapies.

If diagnosed at this premorbid stage, ADHD is most responsive to treatment, and early treatment may also prevent or lessen the impact of comorbid conditions. Early identification and treatment of ADHD, along with monitoring for possible development of comorbid conditions, should be the goal of every clinician working with children with ADHD.

This eBook covers all aspect of ADHD and how it affects a person's mental, psychological and social health. Moreover, ADHD has several types each of which is much more potent than the other. You need to know all signs and symptoms of how and when ADHD starts to develop or when you become prone to it. Also you should know the causes of ADHD occurrence hence to avoid these in future.

ADHD can be treated with conventional treatment that will include stimulating and other medications that temporarily provides a boost to concentration and memory as well as other cognitive functions. Also, ADHD can be treated by several other therapies that are non-medicinal.

The most important part in treating and preventing ADHD is a proper diet. Certain foods can worsen the instance of ADHD while there are others that can be really helpful and cause to take off this burden from your mind. There are a lot of foods that are sensitive to ADHD patients and these must be kept away at all costs. Most importantly, ADHD is greatly dependent on nutritional supplements and vitamins and hence these need to be kept in check.

Made in the USA
Coppell, TX
24 November 2023